Francis Frith's
AROUND MAIDSTONE

PHOTOGRAPHIC MEMORIES

Francis Frith's
AROUND MAIDSTONE

◆

Helen Livingston

FRITH
BOOK Co

First published in the United Kingdom in 1999 by
Frith Book Company Ltd

Hardback Edition 1999
ISBN 1-85937-056-X

Paperback Edition 2001
ISBN 1-85937-391-7

British Library Cataloguing in Publication Data

Around Maidstone
Helen Livingston

Frith Book Company Ltd
Frith's Barn, Teffont,
Salisbury, Wiltshire SP3 5QP
Tel: +44 (0) 1722 716 376
Email: info@francisfrith.co.uk
www.francisfrith.co.uk

Printed and bound in Great Britain

CONTENTS

FRANCIS FRITH: *Victorian Pioneer*

FRANCIS FRITH, Victorian founder of the world-famous photographic archive, was a complex and multitudinous man. A devout Quaker and a highly successful Victorian businessman, he was both philosophic by nature and pioneering in outlook.

By 1855 Francis Frith had already established a wholesale grocery business in Liverpool, and sold it for the astonishing sum of £200,000, which is the equivalent today of over £15,000,000. Now a multi-millionaire, he was able to indulge his passion for travel. As a child he had pored over travel books written by early explorers, and his fancy and imagination had been stirred by family holidays to the sublime mountain regions of Wales and Scotland. 'What a land of spirit-stirring and enriching scenes and places!' he had written. He was to return to these scenes of grandeur in later years to 'recapture the thousands of vivid and tender memories', but with a different purpose. Now in his thirties, and captivated by the new science of photography, Frith set out on a series of pioneering journeys to the Nile regions that occupied him from 1856 until 1860.

INTRIGUE AND ADVENTURE

He took with him on his travels a specially-designed wicker carriage that acted as both dark-room and sleeping chamber. These far-flung journeys were packed with intrigue and adventure. In his life story, written when he was sixty-three, Frith tells of being held captive by bandits, and of fighting 'an awful midnight battle to the very point of surrender with a deadly pack of hungry, wild dogs'. Sporting flowing Arab costume, Frith arrived at Akaba by camel seventy years before Lawrence, where he encountered 'desert princes and rival sheikhs, blazing with jewel-hilted swords'.

During these extraordinary adventures he was assiduously exploring the desert regions bordering the Nile and patiently recording the antiquities and peoples with his camera. He was the first photographer to venture beyond the sixth cataract. Africa was still the mysterious 'Dark Continent', and Stanley and Livingstone's historic meeting was a decade into the future. The conditions for picture taking confound belief. He laboured for hours in his wicker dark-room in the sweltering heat of the desert, while the volatile chemicals fizzed dangerously in their trays. Often he was forced to work in remote tombs and caves where conditions were cooler. Back in London he exhibited his photographs and was 'rapturously cheered' by members of the Royal Society. His reputation as a photographer was made overnight. An eminent modern historian has likened their impact on the population of the time to that on our own generation of the first photographs taken on the surface of the moon.

VENTURE OF A LIFE-TIME

Characteristically, Frith quickly spotted the opportunity to create a new business as a specialist publisher of photographs. He lived in an era of immense and sometimes violent change. For the poor in the early part of Victoria's reign work was a drudge and the hours long, and people had precious little free time to enjoy themselves.

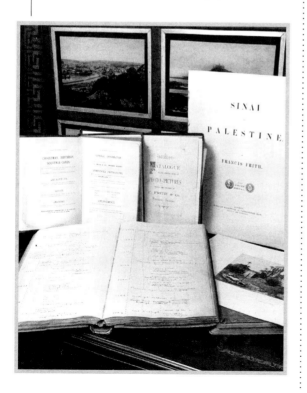

Most had no transport other than a cart or gig at their disposal, and had not travelled far beyond the boundaries of their own town or village. However, by the 1870s, the railways had threaded their way across the country, and Bank Holidays and half-day Saturdays had been made obligatory by Act of Parliament. All of a sudden the ordinary working man and his family were able to enjoy days out and see a little more of the world.

With characteristic business acumen, Francis Frith foresaw that these new tourists would enjoy having souvenirs to commemorate their days out. In 1860 he married Mary Ann Rosling and set out with the intention of photographing every city, town and village in Britain. For the next thirty years he travelled the country by train and by pony and trap, producing fine photographs of seaside resorts and beauty spots that were keenly bought by millions of Victorians. These prints were painstakingly pasted into family albums and pored over during the dark nights of winter, rekindling precious memories of summer excursions.

THE RISE OF FRITH & CO

Frith's studio was soon supplying retail shops all over the country. To meet the demand he gathered about him a small team of photographers, and published the work of independent artist-photographers of the calibre of Roger Fenton and Francis Bedford. In order to gain some understanding of the scale of Frith's business one only has to look at the catalogue issued by Frith & Co in 1886: it runs to some 670

pages, listing not only many thousands of views of the British Isles but also many photographs of most European countries, and China, Japan, the USA and Canada – note the sample page shown above from the hand-written *Frith & Co* ledgers detailing pictures taken. By 1890 Frith had created the greatest specialist photographic publishing company in the world, with over 2,000 outlets – more than the combined number that Boots and WH Smith have today! The picture on the right shows the *Frith & Co* display board at Ingleton in the Yorkshire Dales. Beautifully constructed with mahogany frame and gilt inserts, it could display up to a dozen local scenes.

POSTCARD BONANZA

The ever-popular holiday postcard we know today took many years to develop. In 1870 the Post Office issued the first plain cards, with a pre-printed stamp on one face. In 1894 they allowed other publishers' cards to be sent through the mail with an attached adhesive halfpenny stamp. Demand grew rapidly, and in 1895 a new size of postcard was permitted called the

court card, but there was little room for illustration. In 1899, a year after Frith's death, a new card measuring 5.5 x 3.5 inches became the standard format, but it was not until 1902 that the divided back came into being, with address and message on one face and a full-size illustration on the other. *Frith & Co* were in the vanguard of postcard development, and Frith's sons Eustace and Cyril continued their father's monumental task, expanding the number of views offered to the public and recording more and more places in Britain, as the coasts and countryside were opened up to mass travel.

Francis Frith died in 1898 at his villa in Cannes, his great project still growing. The archive he created continued in business for another seventy years. By 1970 it contained over a third of a million pictures of 7,000 cities, towns and villages. The massive photographic record Frith has left to us stands as a living monument to a special and very remarkable man.

Frith's Archive: *A Unique Legacy*

FRANCIS FRITH'S legacy to us today is of immense significance and value, for the magnificent archive of evocative photographs he created provides a unique record of change in 7,000 cities, towns and villages throughout Britain over a century and more. Frith and his fellow studio photographers revisited locations many times down the years to update their views, compiling for us an enthralling and colourful pageant of British life and character.

We tend to think of Frith's sepia views of Britain as nostalgic, for most of us use them to conjure up memories of places in our own lives with which we have family associations. It often makes us forget that to Francis Frith they were records of daily life as it was actually being lived in the cities, towns and villages of his day. The Victorian age was one of great and often bewildering change for ordinary people, and though the pictures evoke an impression of slower times, life was as busy and hectic as it is today.

We are fortunate that Frith was a photographer of the people, dedicated to recording the minutiae of everyday life. For it is this sheer wealth of visual data, the painstaking chronicle of changes in dress, transport, street layouts, buildings, housing, engineering and landscape that captivates us so much today. His remarkable images offer us a powerful link with the past and with the lives of our ancestors.

TODAY'S TECHNOLOGY

Computers have now made it possible for Frith's many thousands of images to be accessed almost instantly. In the Frith archive today, each photograph is carefully 'digitised' then stored on a CD Rom. Frith archivists can locate a single photograph amongst thousands within seconds. Views can be catalogued and sorted under a variety of categories of place and content to the immediate benefit of researchers. Inexpensive reference prints can be created for them at the touch of a mouse button, and a wide range of books and other printed materials assembled and published for a wider, more general readership - in the next twelve months over a hundred Frith local history titles will be published! The

See Frith at www.francisfrith.co.uk

day-to-day workings of the archive are very different from how they were in Francis Frith's time: imagine the herculean task of sorting through eleven tons of glass negatives as Frith had to do to locate a particular sequence of pictures! Yet the archive still prides itself on maintaining the same high standards of excellence laid down by Francis Frith, including the painstaking cataloguing and indexing of every view.

It is curious to reflect on how the internet now allows researchers in America and elsewhere greater instant access to the archive than Frith himself ever enjoyed. Many thousands of individual views can be called up on screen within seconds on one of the Frith internet sites, enabling people living continents away to revisit the streets of their ancestral home town, or view places in Britain where they have enjoyed holidays. Many overseas researchers welcome the chance to view special theme selections, such as transport, sports, costume and ancient monuments.

We are certain that Francis Frith would have heartily approved of these modern developments, for he himself was always working at the very limits of Victorian photographic technology.

THE VALUE OF THE ARCHIVE TODAY

Because of the benefits brought by the computer, Frith's images are increasingly studied by social historians, by researchers into genealogy and ancestory, by architects, town planners, and by teachers and schoolchildren involved in local history projects. In addition, the archive offers every one of us a unique opportunity to examine the places where we and our families have lived and worked down the years. Immensely successful in Frith's own era, the archive is now, a century and more on, entering a new phase of popularity.

THE PAST IN TUNE WITH THE FUTURE

Historians consider the Francis Frith Collection to be of prime national importance. It is the only archive of its kind remaining in private ownership and has been valued at a million pounds. However, this figure is now rapidly increasing as digital technology enables more and more people around the world to enjoy its benefits.

Francis Frith's archive is now housed in an historic timber barn in the beautiful village of Teffont in Wiltshire. Its founder would not recognize the archive office as it is today. In place of the many thousands of dusty boxes containing glass plate negatives and an all-pervading odour of photographic chemicals, there are now ranks of computer screens. He would be amazed to watch his images travelling round the world at unimaginable speeds through network and internet lines.

The archive's future is both bright and exciting. Francis Frith, with his unshakeable belief in making photographs available to the greatest number of people, would undoubtedly approve of what is being done today with his lifetime's work. His photographs, depicting our shared past, are now bringing pleasure and enlightenment to millions around the world a century and more after his death.

MAIDSTONE – *An Introduction*

MAIDSTONE is Kent's county town, a status that it achieved fairly late in its history. Its position at the very heart of Kent on the banks of the River Medway, Kent's greatest river, helped to ensure that county administration gravitated towards it, and it became the county town in the early 19th century. As a borough, too, Maidstone had been a late starter, receiving its first charter in 1549. It lost the charter briefly in 1554 on account of Wyatt's rebellion, but a new charter was granted by Elizabeth I in 1559. The Town Hall in the High Street dates from 1763.

Maidstone has been a market town since the Middle Ages, with a weekly market held since 1261. As a market town Maidstone owed it prosperity to the surrounding rich farmland and the easy transport on the River Medway. The farms, orchards and hop gardens of the 'Garden of England' could supply the great London market with ease. Today it is an important industrial centre as well as a bustling commercial town with modern shopping centres.

In the 17th and 18th centuries Maidstone's chief industry was the making of linen thread, and its position as chief market town for the region brought it considerable prosperity. Brewing was the major industry during the 19th and early 20th centuries and the heady aroma of malt hung over the town. Paper making was another staple industry, based on the mills at Tovil, once a little village just upstream but now caught up in the spreading urban tentacles of its big sister. By the mid-20th century Maidstone's industries included quarrying, paper making, engineering, printing and fruit and vegetable preserving.

Notwithstanding all this modernity, Maidstone stands on an ancient site. There was a Roman settlement here on the important Roman road connecting the iron workings of the Hastings area with Rochester and the estuaries of the Rivers Medway and Thames. This Roman road has been traced northwards through Maidstone from the cemetery along Lower and Upper Stone Street, Week Street, Scott Street and Albert Street. A Roman cemetery has been found on the Roman road west of Pested Bars Road south of Maidstone cemetery. Ragstone, the distinctive grey sandstone of the Quarry Hills that has contributed such gravity to so many of the area's buildings, has been quarried in the Maidstone area since Roman times.

Maidstone stands on a line of communication even older than the Roman road, the River Medway. This important commercial artery, significant from prehistoric times to the present, can be regarded as the 'highway of Kent'. Maidstone is an historic crossing point, though the river was not bridged here until 1879, when Sir Joseph Bazalgette, who designed London's Embankment, erected the original 'Great Bridge'. Until that time the

used by the Kentish brickworks.

In the Domesday Book Maidstone appears as 'Meddestane', but the derivation of the name is uncertain. It may relate to the River Medway, or it may relate to the Roman road, but has been quoted, most romantically, as being Anglo-Saxon for 'Maiden's Tower', or as 'Mighty Stone Town'. Whatever the truth of the derivation of its name, the town developed at an important crossing point of the River Medway. To the west of the town lies Penenden Heath, an ancient meeting place where shire moots and great assemblies were held and where the first recorded lawsuit in English history took place in 1076. It was also,

Maidstone ferry, which continued to operate well into living memory, was the only means of crossing the river. The River Medway was tidal as far upstream as East Farleigh until the 17th century when the river was controlled by sluices and locks. Today the river is given over to leisure, cruising, angling and rowing. Until the middle years of this century it was a commercial highway plied by tan-sailed Thames barges with their cargoes of timber and paper, and by the 'stumpies', Medway narrow boats

until the 19th century, the scene of public executions. Today it is given over to playing fields. Maidstone was granted to the Archbishop of Canterbury during Norman times, and from the reign of King John until the 16th century was the site of the Primate of All England's country residence. In the Middle Ages it was a small town; the atmosphere of those times still lingers beside the river, where the one-time collegiate church of All Saints and the former Archbishop's Palace form the centre of a well-preserved group of 14th century buildings. Though much of the medieval heart of the town survives, it appears today in isolated buildings and scraps of streets, rather than as a coherent whole. This state of affairs derives from the ring roads, shopping centres and tall office buildings, which between them have shattered the town's once intimate fabric.

Throughout the years Maidstone's citizens have not been afraid to speak their mind, and several national rebellions have been nurtured here. The earliest, the Peasant's Revolt of 1381, was led by two Maidstone men, Wat Tyler and John Ball, 'the mad Priest of Kent'. Ball was imprisoned in the dungeons of the Archbishop's Palace, prior to his public hanging. Maidstone was also the nursery of Jack Cade's 1450 rebellion, and in 1554 bred the ill-fated rising of Sir Thomas Wyatt, a local worthy, who rose against Queen Mary's marriage to Philip II of Spain and lost his head at Tower Hill in consequence. During the Civil War Maidstone was held by Royalist troops loyal to Charles I. On 1 June 1648 the Battle of Maidstone took place, when Sir Thomas Fairfax and a contingent of parliamentary forces forced a crossing of Farleigh Bridge (which was then the nearest bridge across the Medway to Maidstone) and fought their way into the town. A five-hour long battle was fought in the streets, but Fairfax and his men forced a Royalist surrender by midnight the same day. There was particularly fierce fighting in the vicinity of Knightrider Street. A generation later, in 1697, Celia Fiennes, that redoubtable horsewoman and indefatigable traveller, commented with approval that 'Maidstone town is a very neate market town as you shall see in the Country, its buildings

are mostly of timber work'. She went on to remark that 'there are very pretty houses about the town look like the habitations of rich men, I believe it is a wealthy place, there are severall pretty streetes'. Nearly another thirty years later, Daniel Defoe corroborated Miss Fiennes, remarking in his Tour that Maidstone was 'a town of very great business and trade, and yet full of gentry, of mirth and of good company'.

Maidstone began to regard its county town status with a degree of pride during the early 19th century. The original Shire Hall was built in 1824, but changed its function in the early 20th century, becoming the Sessions House when the new County Hall was built. Today most of the county council offices have moved from the town centre to new buildings in the grounds of the Victorian mansion of Springfield, on the Sandling Road.

During the Victorian era Maidstone flourished greatly, though it originally objected to the coming of the railway, and developed into the major manufacturing centre that it remains today. The photographs reproduced in this book take us back to Victorian Maidstone and give us further glimpses of the Maidstone of the early post-War era. Both are vanished worlds. Here is the High Street, with the statue of Queen Victoria only a few years old, and Victorian shop fronts attached to the 18th and early 19th-century buildings. Here it is again, with modern shopfronts and 20th-century traffic of a milder kind than that seen today.

Maidstone has bred several illustrious men. Wat Tyler and John Ball have already been mentioned, as has the luckless Sir Thomas Wyatt, beheaded at Tower Hill. He was a member of a very famous Maidstone family, whose ancestral home was in nearby Allington Castle. His father, another Sir Thomas, was a poet of note in the court of Henry VIII and introduced the sonnet into England. The Wyatts were an important family hereabouts for several generations, and one of their former homes, Chillington Manor in St Faith's Street, is now the museum. During the Wars of the Roses, Sir Henry Wyatt was imprisoned in the tower of London. The tale is told how he was refused food, but was succoured by a friendly cat, who caught pigeons and brought them to him to eat. After he was released, he had his portrait taken with the cat that had saved his life. Other notable Maidstonians include Andrew Broughton, who read the death sentence on Charles I at the King's trial, and William Shipley who founded the Royal Society of Arts in 1754.

William Hazlitt, the essayist, is often claimed as a son of Maidstone, and indeed was born in Earl Street in 1778, but he left the town at the age of two. Disraeli was MP for Maidstone in 1837 and it was here that he anglicised his name by dropping the apostrophe.

Streets and Parks

MAIDSTONE'S street plan has changed dramatically in the second half of the 20th century. New roads impinge on the historic centre of the town and sever the High Street and adjacent streets from the fine complex of buildings surrounding the former Archbishop's Palace beside the River Medway. In this way, modern Maidstone, with its dual carriageways, shopping centre and tower blocks, sits uncomfortably on the vanished Maidstone of the 19th century photographs reproduced here. These show the Victorian town, successor to the county town that so pleased Celia Fiennes in her tour through Kent in 1697. Maidstone, she wrote, 'is a very neate Market towne, its buildings are mostly of timber worke, the streets are large ...' Yet Maidstone has preserved its historic heart astride the spacious High Street on the eastern side of the Medway and much of the 'neate market towne' lingers on.

Maidstone's oldest streets run along the line of the old Roman road which connected Rochester to the iron-mining area inland from Hastings. This highway ran through present day Maidstone along Albert Street, Scott Street, Week Street and Lower and Upper Stone Street to Maidstone Cemetery and beyond. Another ancient route ran westwards down the present-day High Street to the River Medway, where Maidstone Bridge marks the old-established crossing point.

The pictures of Maidstone's historic streets reproduced here include several of the famous High Street and adjacent Bank Street, the latter well-known for its 17th-century buildings, and of Earl Street, known for its colonnaded Market Buildings and the Unitarian church where William Hazlitt's father was minister. Celia Fiennes spoke of the High Street and Market Place with considerable approval: 'this streete,' she wrote, 'notwithstanding the [town] hall and [market] cross stands in the midst, is yet a good breadth on each side and when it comes to meete in one is very broad and runs down a great length, quite to the bridge cross the Medway, which is not very broad here it beares Barges that bring up burdens to the town'. There are several photographs showing the wide High Street during the Victorian era and again in the middle years of the 20th century. Some of these look down towards Maidstone Bridge, where until recent years barges still landed and loaded cargoes at the town quay. In all these pictures the street bustles with activity, an eloquent expression of Maidstone's status as county town. The street that served as the town's market place was formerly very wide along its entire length, but an 'island' block built in the middle has created Bank Street on the southern side. Infilling of wide market places in this way was not unusu-al, and frequently allowed the landowner to make some extra money.

Maidstone is surrounded by the beautiful countryside of the 'garden of England'. To the north of Maidstone near the village of Sandling is Cobtree Manor, known today for its Museum of Kent Life, but for some years formerly home to Maidstone Zoo. Just to the east of the town is Mote Park, an urban park in the grounds of the old mansion of Mote Park. This was bought for the town from Lord Bearsted in 1929 and is famed both for its lake, used for yachting, and for the county cricket ground.

HIGH STREET c1870 1480
This view shows the drinking fountain and statue of Queen Victoria, presented to Maidstone by Alexander Randall, former High Sheriff of Kent, in 1862. To the left is the narrow Bank Street, separated from High Street by a block of buildings that infill the formerly very wide High Street.

MARKET PLACE
1885 12684
This part of the High Street was Maidstone's market place from
early times. The building on the 'island' site with the projecting
clock is the Town Hall of 1762-3.

HIGH STREET c1955 M9004

Looking up a half-deserted High Street on a sunny day. The 'island' block with Bank Street on the right is clearly visible. Numbers 93, 94 and 95 High Street, on the Bank Street side, date from about 1855, an early example of an iron-framed building.

BANK STREET c1955 M9062

This photograph looks down Bank Street towards the High Street and the River Medway. This street is known for its fine timber buildings, many with a conspicuous overhang. There is also some excellent 17th century pargetting (decorated plasterwork); at number 78 it incorporates the arms of Prince Henry, eldest son of James I.

HIGH STREET C1955 M9063
Here we see the High Street from the foot of Bank Street, showing clearly the overhead cables for the trolley-buses, one of which is in the foreground. The Maidstone tramway system opened in 1904, but by 1930 had been replaced by buses and trolleybuses. Maidstone Bridge, which spans the River Medway, lies at the bottom of the hill.

HIGH STREET
c1960 M9090
A more crowded High Street pictured
from nearly the same spot. On the right
is the cannon captured at Sebastopol.

HIGH STREET c1960 M9091

Another view of the High Street looking towards Maidstone Bridge on a sunny spring day. Once known as The Great Bridge, Maidstone Bridge was built in 1879 to designs of Sir Joseph Bazelgette. It was widened in 1927.

THE COLONNADE c1955 M9082

A view of the 19th century colonnade at the Market Buildings in Earl Street. This was built in 1825. To the south is the oldest nonconformist chapel in Maidstone, the Unitarian Church of 1736, where William Hazlitt's father was minister from 1770 to 1780. It is proudly emblazoned with a dated weathervane. The adjacent corn exchange dates from 1835 and is now part of the Hazlitt Theatre Complex.

THE ZOO PARK C1955 M9030

THE ZOO PARK C1955
This zoo, established by the late Sir
Garrard Tyrwhitt-Drake, formerly stood
in the grounds of Cobtree Manor. It was
known for its well-kept lions and
polar bears.

THE ZOO PARK C1955
One of Maidstone Zoo's zebras. The
grounds of Cobtree Manor, at Sandling,
close to Maidstone, now house the
Museum of Kent Life, Cobtree Manor
Golf Course and a 250 acre park.

THE ZOO PARK C1955 M9039

MOTE PARK c1955 M9071
This country house, now a Cheshire Home, was built in 1793-1801 by the architect D A Alexander, who later built Maidstone and Dartmoor prisons. Old Mote House, its predecessor, was the childhood home of Elizabeth Woodville (1437-1492), mother of the 'princes in the tower'.

MOTE PARK, THE LAKE c1955 M9028
The grounds of Mote Park have been used as a public park for many years. The park covers some 558 acres and now includes a nature trail, model car racing track, pitch and putt and a children's playground as well a miniature railway in the summer.

MOTE PARK c1965 M9102
The lake was created in the mid-18th century by damming the little river Len, which flows into the Medway near the Archbishop's Palace. Maidstone Leisure Centre is situated in Mote Park.

Churches and Notable Buildings

UP UNTIL the Second World War Maidstone was a compact town of three-storied buildings and narrow streets. Much of the architecture possessed a distinctive Kentish 'feel', built of local materials: brick and ragstone. Today many of these buildings have been demolished. Tower blocks overshadow much of the town that remains and dwarf the earlier buildings, so they are seemingly cowering at the prospect of their own probable fate.

Many of Maidstone's older buildings have been demolished, but several notable ones remain. The churches pictured here are Archbishop Courtenay's famous collegiate church of All Saints and the Victorian church of St Faith, which was built on the site of an earlier chapel. All Saints is the largest parish church in Kent, 227 feet long, and dates from 1395 when the original church on the site was completely rebuilt by Archbishop Courtenay. This was done at the same time as the building of the college, for the pope had just given authority for the church at Maidstone to be made collegiate.

All Saints' Church is one of the large group of medieval buildings, in sombre Kentish ragstone, that form a picturesque group beside the River Medway. The chief building is the former Archbishop's Palace, the oldest building in Maidstone. The original mansion was given in 1205 by the Rector of Maidstone, William de Cornhill, to Archbishop Stephen Langton. Part of this Norman building survives, but it was largely rebuilt in the 14th century as a suitable residence for the Archbishop of Canterbury, and was used as a stopping-off point for journeys between London and Canterbury. The Palace and College of Priests passed out of ecclesiastical hands in 1537. In the early 17th century it belonged to the Astley family, who added the present east front. It is an interesting design. The central two-storied porch is in fact blind, and the two flanking porches, entered up flights of steps, give access to the first floor. Along the River Medway the Palace seems to rise from the water, which makes it appear much taller than it is, and provides one of the most photographed and attractive pictures of Maidstone. In 1909 the old sash windows were replaced by 'authentic' stone mullioned ones. The palace is now a heritage centre with interpretative displays about the households and lives of the Archbishops of

Canterbury who lived here.

Other buildings in the church and palace riverside group include some remaining fragments of the college of priests, chiefly the gatehouse and the master's house, the Archbishop's stables and the little palace gatehouse. This last was probably originally a millhouse at the confluence of the river Medway and its tributary the River Len. It became the gatehouse to the palace of the Archbishop of Canterbury during the 14th century. It is now used as the tourist information centre.

Another famous Maidstone building is the Museum in St Faith's Street. This was Chillington Manor House, a former home of the Wyatts. It is a splendid red brick 16th-century house with magnificent Tudor chimneys and an early Tudor long gallery. The central portion of the house was built during Elizabethan times by Nicholas Barham, Maidstone's first MP.

ST FAITH'S CHURCH 1892 31496
St Faith's is one of Maidstone's Victorian churches. The church was built in Kentish ragstone in 1872 on the site of a medieval chapel. The tower was built in 1880-81, but the pinnacles were removed for safety reasons in 1938.

ST FAITH'S CHURCH 1898 41541
Another picture of St Faith's Church, taken six years after the previous photograph. The trees have grown and the whole scene looks more rural.

ALL SAINTS CHURCH 1892 31487

This is the largest parish church in Kent, 227 feet long, and dates from 1395 when the original church on the site was completely rebuilt by Archbishop Courtenay. This was done at the same time as the building of the college. The college buildings are to the right of the church.

ALL SAINTS CHURCH 1898 41528

This photograph is taken from across the River Medway and showing Victorians strolling along the Undercliff walk and the 'horseway' path down to the river Medway, and Victorian children leaning on the railings watching the river - and maybe the photographer on the opposite bank!

ALL SAINTS CHURCH
1898 41529

This is the last resting place of William Grocyn (died 1519), a friend of the great humanist Erasmus and master of the college of priests. In the churchyard is the tomb of William Shipley, founder of the Royal Society of Arts.

THE PARISH CHURCH c1955 M9007
Looking across the River Medway to the tower of All Saints' Church. The church originally had a spire, but this was struck by lightning and destroyed in 1730.

ALL SAINTS CHURCH 1892 31488
The aisled nave is 93ft wide and is covered by a magnificent vaulted roof in oak, installed by Pearson during his 1886 restoration. This view looks down the spacious nave and shows the wide nave aisles. The high arches of the nave arcades echo the proportions of Canterbury cathedral.

ALL SAINTS CHURCH 1898 41530
The octagonal Jacobean font is decorated with the arms of Scotland, Ireland, Maidstone and the Astley family, who were granted the former Archbishop's Palace in Elizabethan times. The font is made of Sussex marble.

ALL SAINTS CHURCH 1898 41531
This view shows the church screen. Laurence Washington, great uncle of George, who died in 1619, is buried in the church. His memorial in the south aisle is emblazoned with the stars and stripes which were to be perpetuated in the United States' flag.

THE OLD PALACE 1892 31490

THE OLD PALACE 1892

The east front of the Archbishop's Palace, pictured prior to the insertion of the modern window and the change in the roofline of the central porch. This front was built in the early 17th century. Access to the first floor is via the two outer porchways up flights of steps, and the central two-storied porch is blind. Access to the ground floor is via the door to the right of the central porch.

◆

THE ARCHBISHOP'S PALACE 1898

This view shows the alteration of the window and roofline of the central porch. The palace is Maidstone's oldest building, originally Norman, but substantially rebuilt in the 14th century. The Palace and College of Priests passed out of ecclesiastical hands in 1537.

THE ARCHBISHOP'S PALACE 1898 41534

THE ARCHBISHOP'S PALACE 1898 41533
Looking across the tranquil River Medway to the Archbishop's Palace
and the Undercliff Walk. The picture was taken prior to the
replacement of the old sash windows by 'authentic' stone mullioned
ones in 1909. In 1887 the grounds were bought by public
subscription to commemorate Queen Victoria's jubilee, and the
palace itself was later restored by Maidstone
Borough Council.

THE ARCHBISHOP'S PALACE c1955 M9074
Swans line the riverbank looking towards the Archbishop's Palace, where people enjoy the sun on the Undercliff
Walk.

COLLEGE GATE 1898 41540
Here we see the impressive battlemented three-storeyed gatehouse of Archbishop Courtenay's college for a master
and twenty-four chaplains. The tower of All Saints is in the centre of the picture.

THE TITHE BARN C1955 M9015
The former stables of the Archbishop's Palace, for long believed to be a tithe barn. The building now houses the famous Tyrwhitt-Drake Museum of Carriages.

THE OLD HOUSE, CHATHAM ROAD c1965 M9134

This is Old Farm House, an old Wealden-type hall house on Chatham Road. This house has been restored and is typical of 15th-century building in the wooded Weald.

THE MUSEUM 1892 31491

Maidstone Museum occupies the former home of the Wyatts, Chillington Manor House, a splendid red brick Tudor house. This view is taken from Brenchley Gardens, an oasis of peace and quiet near the very heart of town. The gardens were given to Maidstone in 1873 by Julius Lucius Brenchley. There is a Victorian bandstand at which concerts are still given on Sunday afternoons in summer.

THE MUSEUM 1898 41543
The courtyard, with the then-pinnacled tower of St Faith's visible in the background. The museum houses outstanding collections, including the museum of the Queen's Own West Kent Regiment, archaeology, Egyptology, ceramics, costumes, Japanese artefacts, ethnography and natural history.

THE MUSEUM 1898 41542
This view shows the magnificent Tudor chimneys of the Museum. The early Tudor long gallery was preserved when the central portion was built during Elizabethan times by Nicholas Barham, Maidstone's first MP.

KENT COUNTY LIBRARY c1965 M9139
Kent's central lending library is at Springfields. This is one of modern Maidstone's many tower blocks. The building is twelve storeys high, and houses the support collection for the whole of Kent as well as specialist collections of music, drama and recorded sound and a large general collection.

The River Medway

MAIDSTONE turns her best face to the River Medway on whose banks she lies. Just above Maidstone Bridge is the pleasant Undercliff Walk backed by the remarkable group of mellow medieval buildings centred on All Saints Church, the former Archbishop's Palace and the associated college of priests. The view, particularly when seen from the towpath along the river bank, gives the impression that Maidstone is a well-preserved medieval town. This quality is emphasised by the late 19th-century photographs given here. These photographs also show that downstream of Maidstone Bridge, a structure dating from 1879 and widened in 1927 and which stands at the traditional crossing point of the river, comes industrial Maidstone with wharves, chimneys and noise. One feature not shown in these pictures is St Peter's Bridge, a new bridge over the river that was built in 1978.

The River Medway bisects the county into its traditional halves, with 'Kentish men' living to its west and 'men of Kent' to its east. Although arguably the most Kentish of all rivers, the Medway rises in Sussex, its headwaters a group of little streams on the heathy heights of Ashdown Forest, one time centre of the Wealden iron industry. It flows through the Weald and past Maidstone to the Thames estuary, and was for many years under the jurisdiction of the Mayor and Corporation of the City of London, who combined its administration with that of the River Thames.

The River Medway has long been known as two rivers; the upper reaches fertile and rural, flowing through the 'Garden of England', the lower reaches, below Maidstone Bridge, mostly industrial, with breweries, paper works, engineering works, quarries and gravel pits lining its banks. This distinction is only partly true, and it must be remembered that in times gone by, when the roads of Kent were quagmires for several months of the year, the River Medway was Kent's great highway. Wealden timber and ordnance (cannon balls in particular) were shipped downstream to Chatham and its great dockyard to help fight Philip of Spain and later Napoleon. Bricks made from Wealden clay, and building stone from the quarries near Maidstone, were carried downriver to rebuild London after the Great Fire of 1666. Fruit, hops, corn and other agricultural produce were despatched by ship to the London market. Trade upstream consisted largely of coal from northern England. Some of the photographs in this book show a vanished Medway, with timber rafts towed by barges outside the Archbishop's palace, a once-familiar scene of the river as an industrial highway that is no more.

Maidstone was the head of navigation of the Medway for centuries. This was because the river's upper reaches were crowded with fisheries and mills that impeded navigation. None the less, by the 1580s the river could be navigated as far upstream as Yalding, six miles above Maidstone. The clearance of the navigation was a very contentious issue in the early 17th century and an Act enabling the building of locks and wharves was not passed until 1664. The navigation was continued upstream to Tonbridge in 1749 and fourteen locks created. The first to be built was at Maidstone.

Allington Lock, the lowest of ten on the river today, was originally built in 1792. The lock was enlarged in 1881 and replaced in 1939. Below Allington Lock the Medway is tidal and the character of the river is very different, with a wide expanse of black mud exposed at low tide. A flood control barrier has been constructed next to the lock in a bid to halt the bad flooding which has periodically occurred in the Medway valley. These photographs include an evocative Victorian picture of Allington Lock.

The navigation was created for commerce, but today the Medway at Maidstone is essentially a recreational river. Several of these photographs show this aspect, with rowing boats for hire below the Archbishop's Palace, and pleasure boats and cruisers plying the river. Every July Maidstone holds a River Festival.

ALL SAINTS CHURCH 1862 1481
This photograph is taken from across the Medway, looking towards All Saints Church and the College. Logs and sawn timber await at the wharf for shipment along the river - in this view empty of barges. This view was taken prior to the building of Maidstone Bridge in 1879.

ALL SAINTS CHURCH 1892 31483
A similar view taken thirty years later, showing the river Medway as an industrial highway. Barges towing rafts of sawn timber head past the Archbishop's Palace and All Saints Church. Formerly, a ferry crossed the Medway at this point.

ALL SAINTS CHURCH
1892 31484
A tranquil view of the deserted Medway with the reflections
of All Saints Church and the Archbishop's Palace hardly
stirring on a warm windless day. People relax on the benches
along Undercliff Walk.

THE PROMENADE AND THE BRIDGE 1898 41535
The promenade - Undercliff Walk - alongside the Archbishop's Palace, looking north towards Maidstone Bridge and the chimneys of the industrial area beyond.

ALL SAINTS CHURCH 1898 41527
Another evocative view of the Medway, this time looking downstream round the meander bend. The quiet scene belies the nearness of the industrial town.

ALLINGTON LOCKS 1898 41548
Allington Locks, a popular spot with locals and visitors alike, were built in 1792 and enlarged in 1881. The locks pictured here were replaced in 1939. In this picture the riverside inn, the Malta, lies to the right. Today traditional barges are moored along this reach, and in summer months a 'river bus' operates a regular service from the Malta Inn to Maidstone.

THE RIVER MEDWAY C1955 M9018
The busy river: this view shows both its commercial and leisure aspects. A barge loads at the quay, pleasure boats take trippers for a cruise.

THE RIVER MEDWAY c1955 M9025
The recreational river: this view shows the bustling Undercliff Walk, with rowing boats for hire. A trip on the river was particularly popular at this time.

THE RIVER MEDWAY c1955 M9087
Swans are afloat on the river on a sunny day. The wooded nature of the river banks is noticeable, and only the industrial scene on the far right of the picture would suggest that this is near the centre of a busy modern industrial town.

ALL SAINTS CHURCH
c1955 M9073
The swans preen themselves on the river bank looking across to the church. There are nearly always swans on the Medway at Maidstone. They add a dignified dimension to the scene, set against the mellow grouping of the Archbishop's Palace, All Saints Church and the College.

THE RIVER MEDWAY c1955 M9020
A wintry scene, showing the Archbishop's Palace and the tower of All Saints Church. The boats are moored at the quayside

THE RIVER MEDWAY c1965
Rowers speed past moored motor cruisers on a sylvan reach of the river, close to the town centre.

◆

FROM THE BRIDGE c1965
Pleasure craft are moored alongside the Archbishop's Palace. This picture shows the transformation of the River Medway into a recreational highway rather than a commercial one.

THE RIVER MEDWAY c1965 M9117

FROM THE BRIDGE c1965 M9118

Nearby Villages and Sights

MAIDSTONE is the administrative capital of Kent, the oldest county in the history of England. The name 'Kent' derives from the 'Cantii', the Belgic tribe that inhabited the region at the time of the Roman invasions. The Medway has traditionally divided Kent into two halves: the 'men of Kent' to the east and 'Kentish men' to the west. This corner of England has been important since time immemorial, strategically, spiritually and industrially. These photos capture the historic importance of this corner of ancient Kent.

About three miles to the north of Maidstone are the North Downs. Situated up on the crest of this chalk ridge are some of the oldest monuments in England, the prehistoric long barrows and tumuli marking the burial sites of a long-forgotten people. The most famous, Kits Coty House, is seen here, with its massive cap stone. There are other monuments nearby, including Little Kits Coty and the White Horse Stone, whilst some miles to the east are the Coldrum Stones.

The Medway has been a strategically important river since early days, and Aylesford, just to the north of Maidstone, is believed to have been the site of a pitched bat-tle between the invading Saxons and the Celtic tribes who used to inhabit the Kentish Kingdom. It has remained a river of strategic importance. This is reflected in the Castle at Allington, hard by the Medway, which was important in medieval times. A few miles to the east of Maidstone is Leeds Castle, believed to have been founded by the Saxons, which is romantically situated on a lake on the River Len.

Kent was the cradle of English Christianity, following the conversion of the Kentish Kingdom by St Augustine in AD 597, nearly 200 years after the end of Roman rule in Britain. The ecclesiastical centres have always been at Canterbury and Rochester, but the Kentish churches and religious foundations have been well-known since those days. The Carmelite friary at Aylesford was founded in medieval days and flourished until the dissolution. The friary became private property for about 400 years, but was re-purchased by the Carmelites just after the last war. Today, it is once again an important religious centre and a place of pilgrimage. Aside from the friary, there are some particularly fine churches dating back to Saxon and Norman days, and the

Frith photographers recorded three of these, at Bearsted, Aylesford and Leeds.

Industry has never been far away from this area. The Medway valley and those of its tributaries have been the home all sorts of activities and trades. From the middle ages to the 19th century, the rivers powered a considerable number of mills, and in these pictures can be seen some of the half dozen or so mills which once spun wool in the Loose valley, just to the south of Maidstone on the River Loose.

The villages and hamlets surrounding Maidstone are particularly attractive. Since some of the earlier pictures in this collection were taken, Maidstone and some of the surrounding villages have grown in size. Some of the places pictured here, for example the pleasing village of Loose, have now been swallowed by 'greater' Maidstone. Aylesford still retains its attractive independence, although the medieval bridge seen here has now been joined by an altogether newer affair. Its houses and inns are ancient. The deep peace of such places as Aylesford, as recorded by these Victorian photographers, has been disturbed, at least for the present, by the roads and motorways.

AYLESFORD, THE VILLAGE AND THE BRIDGE C1960 A85009
The bridge at Aylesford has long been an important crossing point on the Medway. The bridge is on the site of an ancient ford, once the only crossing between Rochester and Maidstone. The bridge dates from medieval times, but has been restored subsequently. In this view, the elegant proportions of the bridge are much in evidence.

AYLESFORD, GENERAL VIEW
1898 41549
Aylesford is a quaint, rather old-fashioned village perfectly situated on the
Medway about three miles north of Maidstone. The village was the scene of
many battles in ancient years. The Carmelite friary, rededicated in 1949, is now
a place of pilgrimage. It also has an industrial side, which includes a substantial
paper mill. In this view, the tidal Medway is clearly seen, together with Medway
sailing barges drawn up in the tidal mud.

AYLESFORD, THE BRIDGE c1960 A85045

Another fine view, this time taken at high tide. The river washes the quayside above the bridge. The Church of St Peter dominates the scene.

AYLESFORD, THE BRIDGE c1960 A85053

A close-up of the bridge taken downsteam of the previous pictures. There is a magnificent prospect of the church, which looks over the eight brick gables of the cottages. The bridge is built of ragstone and dates from the 14th century. A further bridge has been built since these photos were taken.

AYLESFORD, THE VILLAGE c1960 A85080
A close-up of the cottages nestling by the side of the River Medway, with St Peter's Church in the background. Although this scene appears tranquil, the railway line runs close to the river here, and now the M2 motorway runs only a short distance further south.

AYLESFORD, THE RIVER c1960
This photograph shows a quintessential English village scene in summer. The village cottages and houses crowd down to the river, surrounded by luxuriant vegetation. St Peter's Church stands guardian on its knoll.

AYLESFORD, THE CHURCH c1960
A close-up of St Peter's Church, which dates from Norman times, although it is mostly medieval. In the foreground is a stair-turret to the rood-loft.

AYLESFORD, THE RIVER c1960 A85049

AYLESFORD, THE CHURCH c1960 A85058

AYLESFORD, THE CHURCH c1960 A85073
This view emphasises the fine proportions of the church, with its west tower of ragstone, together with its stair turret. In the foreground can be seen the old churchyard.

AYLESFORD, CAGE HILL c1960 A85071
Aylesford is a knot of twisting streets, clinging to the side of the valley. In this view of the road near the church, the quiet nature of the road is clearly visible, recalling a typical village scene before the car began to strangle the English village.

AYLESFORD, THE BRIDGE AND HIGH STREET C1960 A85078
A wonderfully evocative village scene. This view is taken from the bridge, looking into the village. The narrow width of the medieval bridge is clearly seen, which even then required traffic lights to regulate the flow of vehicles. The noticeboards on the left speak of an era now disappeared.

AYLESFORD, THE ALMSHOUSES C1960 A85050
These houses, also known as the Hospital of the Holy Trinity, were founded in the 17th century. Built in ragstone, these pleasant cottages with dormers were restored in about 1842. They were extended at one end at the close of the Victorian era.

AYLESFORD
The Chequers Inn 1960 A85013
The Chequers is a large, commodious old inn, on three storeys with a plastered front. In those days, the inn was owned by Fremlins, a brewer based in Maidstone, which some years later became part of the Whitbread empire.

AYLESFORD, KITS COTY HOUSE 1898 41555

Kits Coty House, a prehistoric burial monument, is sited on a crest of the North Downs a mile or two to the north of Aylesford village. There are three upright stones, covered by a cap stone about 13ft long. In this picture the monument was even then surrounded by iron railings to protect it from visitors. Today the Pilgrim's Way, a well-known long-distance path, runs nearby and there are many more visitors than when this photograph was taken.

AYLESFORD, PRESTON HALL 1898 41552

Preston Hall is situated about half a mile south of Aylesford. It was built for Edward Betts in about 1850. Architecturally, the result is not altogether pleasing, but this view shows its sprawling skyline to perfection. Since these pictures were taken, it has become a chest hospital.

AYLESFORD, PRESTON HALL AND THE FOUNTAIN 1898 41554
The fountain was carved by the architect John Thomas in 1851. He was sculptor to Prince Albert, and the Fountain is one of the more successful aspects of the design of the house. Note the tower to the right of the main building.

Bearsted, The Village
1898 41565

Bearsted is an attractive village that nestles around its ancient green. Formerly the scene of Civil War skirmishes, it is now famous in cricket history. This view shows the attractive nature of Bearsted's village green, grazed contentedly when the photographer visited by cattle and horses. The winding path across the green leads the eye to the distant tower of the Norman church.

BEARSTED, THE CHURCH 1898 41566
The Church is Norman, and this picture shows its tower which is crowned with some curious sculptures of lions.
The church also possesses a massive timbered roof.

LOOSE, THE VILLAGE 1898 41560
The little village of Loose, pronounced 'Luse', is pleasantly situated on the little river of the same name just to the south of Maidstone. Although it is close to Maidstone, it has preserved its character, and sports pretty timbered and tile-hung houses. This excellent view details the handsome little village, with the church huddled among the trees in the distance.

LOOSE, LITTLE IVY MILL 1898 41562
There were once various mills situated on the river at Loose. Note the laden waggons in the foreground, redolent of a long-vanished rural scene.

LOOSE, GREAT IVY MILL
1898 41563
This charming picture of the mill, taken from the
mill-pond, shows that Great Ivy Mill is an altogether more
substantial affair than the mill in the previous picture,
and that it sports a chimney.

ALLINGTON, THE CASTLE 1898 41546
Allington is a hamlet on the Medway just to the north of Maidstone. It is best known for its castle, situated hard by the River Medway. This view shows the excellent defensive site of the castle. Today, this area is rather overshadowed by the motorway, which runs just to the right of the picture.

ALLINGTON, THE CASTLE 1898 41547
The ivy gives the castle a romantic air. This site has been in constant habitation since earliest days, and there was a moated village here before the Romans came. In Tudor times, the castle became the home of the Wyatt family.

AYLESFORD, THE FRIARY, ORIGINAL BUILDINGS c1960 A85032
The Carmelite friary was founded in 1242 when the first Carmelites arrived from the Holy Land. They stayed here until the Dissolution of the Monasteries three hundred years later. Four hundred years after it was dissolved, the Carmelites returned. This picture shows part of the remains of the foundations of the original building. The small scale of the earlier buildings when compared to those built later is striking.

AYLESFORD, THE FRIARY COURTYARD c1960 A85022

AYLESFORD
The Friary Courtyard c1960
The friary is situated on the outskirts of
Aylesford village. It was dissolved by
Henry VIII, but the Carmelites returned
in 1949 and set about rebuilding their
old monastery. Today, it is an intriguing
mixture of old and new architecture.

AYLESFORD
The Friary Courtyard c1960
All is quiet except for a friar crossing the
courtyard. Most of the buildings date
from the 14th and 15th centuries, but
there are traces going back to medieval
times. The Pilgrim's Hall is little altered
from the 15th century.

AYLESFORD, THE FRIARY COURTYARD c1960 A85023

LEEDS CASTLE, THE COURTYARD 1892 31501

The small village of Leeds is dominated by the presence of its large romantic castle. The Castle is Norman, but there was an earlier Saxon castle on the site. The Castle remained a royal palace for centuries afterwards. It eventually became a private residence, and was left to the nation in 1974. Since then it has become a full blooded tourist attraction, set in its 500 acre park. This view shows the Courtyard and the main entrance to the Castle.

LEEDS CASTLE 1892 31500

A famous view of Leeds Castle rising serenely from its two islands in a lake on the river Len. At that time, it was still a private residence, its past as a 'queen's castle' and a prison for 'persons of consequence' but a distant memory. This view shows the magnificent main building and the Gloirette, a D-shaped 'annex' linked to the main building by a double-story bridge.

LEEDS CASTLE
Constable Gate 1892 31502
The main entrance to Leeds Castle was then known as
the Constable Gate. In this picture, the massive
proportions of the Gate Tower are clearly seen. The
ivy-clad building has long since been cleaned, so that
today the Castle displays a less romantic image.

LEEDS CASTLE 1892 31498

A superb view of the main building and the Gloirette. Although the Castle appears to be medieval, its turrets and battlements in fact date from a rebuilding in the late 1820s. The lake is part of the river Len.

LEEDS CASTLE 1892 31503

This view looks towards the Gloirette; on the left can be seen the main building. In this picture, the magnificent location of the Castle, surrounded by its enchanting lake, is clearly seen.

LEEDS CASTLE 1898 41568

A wonderful view of the Castle, showing to advantage the main building and the Gloirette, as well as the Maiden Tower, just visible on the left hand side as the lake swings round to the Gate Tower. Unusually for photographs of the time, the clouds are seen to good effect.

LEEDS CASTLE c1955 M9079

The main building dominates the picture, together with the Gloirette on the left. At this time, the castle was still in private hands. Today, the scene is altogether cleaner and tidier, but perhaps lacks the charm shown in this photograph.

LEEDS CASTLE
1898 41569
The photographer has emphasised the romantic aspect of
the Castle, which is reckoned to be perhaps the most
beautiful castle in the world. The wooden gate and fence add
old-fashioned charm to this view.

LEEDS CASTLE
The Church 1892 31505
The church is dedicated to St Nicholas. The Church has
traces of Saxon and Norman work. This view emphasises
the massive west tower, together with the various
additions to the nave.

Index

Frith Book Co Titles

www.francisfrith.co.uk

The Frith Book Company publishes over 100 new titles each year. A selection of those currently available are listed below. For latest catalogue please contact Frith Book Co.

Town Books 96pages, approx 100 photos. County and Themed Books 128 pages, approx 150 photos (unless specified). All titles hardback laminated case and jacket except those indicated pb (paperback).

Amersham, Chesham & Rickmansworth (pb)			Derby (pb)	1-85937-367-4	£9.99
	1-85937-340-2	£9.99	Derbyshire (pb)	1-85937-196-5	£9.99
Ancient Monuments & Stone Circles	1-85937-143-4	£17.99	Devon (pb)	1-85937-297-x	£9.99
Aylesbury (pb)	1-85937-227-9	£9.99	Dorset (pb)	1-85937-269-4	£9.99
Bakewell	1-85937-113-2	£12.99	Dorset Churches	1-85937-172-8	£17.99
Barnstaple (pb)	1-85937-300-3	£9.99	Dorset Coast (pb)	1-85937-299-6	£9.99
Bath (pb)	1-85937419-0	£9.99	Dorset Living Memories	1-85937-210-4	£14.99
Bedford (pb)	1-85937-205-8	£9.99	Down the Severn	1-85937-118-3	£14.99
Berkshire (pb)	1-85937-191-4	£9.99	Down the Thames (pb)	1-85937-278-3	£9.99
Berkshire Churches	1-85937-170-1	£17.99	Down the Trent	1-85937-311-9	£14.99
Blackpool (pb)	1-85937-382-8	£9.99	Dublin (pb)	1-85937-231-7	£9.99
Bognor Regis (pb)	1-85937-431-x	£9.99	East Anglia (pb)	1-85937-265-1	£9.99
Bournemouth	1-85937-067-5	£12.99	East London	1-85937-080-2	£14.99
Bradford (pb)	1-85937-204-x	£9.99	East Sussex	1-85937-130-2	£14.99
Brighton & Hove(pb)	1-85937-192-2	£8.99	Eastbourne	1-85937-061-6	£12.99
Bristol (pb)	1-85937-264-3	£9.99	Edinburgh (pb)	1-85937-193-0	£8.99
British Life A Century Ago (pb)	1-85937-213-9	£9.99	England in the 1880s	1-85937-331-3	£17.99
Buckinghamshire (pb)	1-85937-200-7	£9.99	English Castles (pb)	1-85937-434-4	£9.99
Camberley (pb)	1-85937-222-8	£9.99	English Country Houses	1-85937-161-2	£17.99
Cambridge (pb)	1-85937-422-0	£9.99	Essex (pb)	1-85937-270-8	£9.99
Cambridgeshire (pb)	1-85937-420-4	£9.99	Exeter	1-85937-126-4	£12.99
Canals & Waterways (pb)	1-85937-291-0	£9.99	Exmoor	1-85937-132-9	£14.99
Canterbury Cathedral (pb)	1-85937-179-5	£9.99	Falmouth	1-85937-066-7	£12.99
Cardiff (pb)	1-85937-093-4	£9.99	Folkestone (pb)	1-85937-124-8	£9.99
Carmarthenshire	1-85937-216-3	£14.99	Glasgow (pb)	1-85937-190-6	£9.99
Chelmsford (pb)	1-85937-310-0	£9.99	Gloucestershire	1-85937-102-7	£14.99
Cheltenham (pb)	1-85937-095-0	£9.99	Great Yarmouth (pb)	1-85937-426-3	£9.99
Cheshire (pb)	1-85937-271-6	£9.99	Greater Manchester (pb)	1-85937-266-x	£9.99
Chester	1-85937-090-x	£12.99	Guildford (pb)	1-85937-410-7	£9.99
Chesterfield	1-85937-378-x	£9.99	Hampshire (pb)	1-85937-279-1	£9.99
Chichester (pb)	1-85937-228-7	£9.99	Hampshire Churches (pb)	1-85937-207-4	£9.99
Colchester (pb)	1-85937-188-4	£8.99	Harrogate	1-85937-423-9	£9.99
Cornish Coast	1-85937-163-9	£14.99	Hastings & Bexhill (pb)	1-85937-131-0	£9.99
Cornwall (pb)	1-85937-229-5	£9.99	Heart of Lancashire (pb)	1-85937-197-3	£9.99
Cornwall Living Memories	1-85937-248-1	£14.99	Helston (pb)	1-85937-214-7	£9.99
Cotswolds (pb)	1-85937-230-9	£9.99	Hereford (pb)	1-85937-175-2	£9.99
Cotswolds Living Memories	1-85937-255-4	£14.99	Herefordshire	1-85937-174-4	£14.99
County Durham	1-85937-123-x	£14.99	Hertfordshire (pb)	1-85937-247-3	£9.99
Croydon Living Memories	1-85937-162-0	£9.99	Horsham (pb)	1-85937-432-8	£9.99
Cumbria	1-85937-101-9	£14.99	Humberside	1-85937-215-5	£14.99
Dartmoor	1-85937-145-0	£14.99	Hythe, Romney Marsh & Ashford	1-85937-256-2	£9.99

Available from your local bookshop or from the publisher

Frith Book Co Titles (continued)

Ipswich (pb)	1-85937-424-7	£9.99	St Ives (pb)	1-85937415-8	£9.99
Ireland (pb)	1-85937-181-7	£9.99	Scotland (pb)	1-85937-182-5	£9.99
Isle of Man (pb)	1-85937-268-6	£9.99	Scottish Castles (pb)	1-85937-323-2	£9.99
Isles of Scilly	1-85937-136-1	£14.99	Sevenoaks & Tunbridge	1-85937-057-8	£12.99
Isle of Wight (pb)	1-85937-429-8	£9.99	Sheffield, South Yorks (pb)	1-85937-267-8	£9.99
Isle of Wight Living Memories	1-85937-304-6	£14.99	Shrewsbury (pb)	1-85937-325-9	£9.99
Kent (pb)	1-85937-189-2	£9.99	Shropshire (pb)	1-85937-326-7	£9.99
Kent Living Memories	1-85937-125-6	£14.99	Somerset	1-85937-153-1	£14.99
Lake District (pb)	1-85937-275-9	£9.99	South Devon Coast	1-85937-107-8	£14.99
Lancaster, Morecambe & Heysham (pb)	1-85937-233-3	£9.99	South Devon Living Memories	1-85937-168-x	£14.99
Leeds (pb)	1-85937-202-3	£9.99	South Hams	1-85937-220-1	£14.99
Leicester	1-85937-073-x	£12.99	Southampton (pb)	1-85937-427-1	£9.99
Leicestershire (pb)	1-85937-185-x	£9.99	Southport (pb)	1-85937-425-5	£9.99
Lincolnshire (pb)	1-85937-433-6	£9.99	Staffordshire	1-85937-047-0	£12.99
Liverpool & Merseyside (pb)	1-85937-234-1	£9.99	Stratford upon Avon	1-85937-098-5	£12.99
London (pb)	1-85937-183-3	£9.99	Suffolk (pb)	1-85937-221-x	£9.99
Ludlow (pb)	1-85937-176-0	£9.99	Suffolk Coast	1-85937-259-7	£14.99
Luton (pb)	1-85937-235-x	£9.99	Surrey (pb)	1-85937-240-6	£9.99
Maidstone	1-85937-056-x	£14.99	Sussex (pb)	1-85937-184-1	£9.99
Manchester (pb)	1-85937-198-1	£9.99	Swansea (pb)	1-85937-167-1	£9.99
Middlesex	1-85937-158-2	£14.99	Tees Valley & Cleveland	1-85937-211-2	£14.99
New Forest	1-85937-128-0	£14.99	Thanet (pb)	1-85937-116-7	£9.99
Newark (pb)	1-85937-366-6	£9.99	Tiverton (pb)	1-85937-178-7	£9.99
Newport, Wales (pb)	1-85937-258-9	£9.99	Torbay	1-85937-063-2	£12.99
Newquay (pb)	1-85937-421-2	£9.99	Truro	1-85937-147-7	£12.99
Norfolk (pb)	1-85937-195-7	£9.99	Victorian and Edwardian Cornwall	1-85937-252-x	£14.99
Norfolk Living Memories	1-85937-217-1	£14.99	Victorian & Edwardian Devon	1-85937-253-8	£14.99
Northamptonshire	1-85937-150-7	£14.99	Victorian & Edwardian Kent	1-85937-149-3	£14.99
Northumberland Tyne & Wear (pb)	1-85937-281-3	£9.99	Vic & Ed Maritime Album	1-85937-144-2	£17.99
North Devon Coast	1-85937-146-9	£14.99	Victorian and Edwardian Sussex	1-85937-157-4	£14.99
North Devon Living Memories	1-85937-261-9	£14.99	Victorian & Edwardian Yorkshire	1-85937-154-x	£14.99
North London	1-85937-206-6	£14.99	Victorian Seaside	1-85937-159-0	£17.99
North Wales (pb)	1-85937-298-8	£9.99	Villages of Devon (pb)	1-85937-293-7	£9.99
North Yorkshire (pb)	1-85937-236-8	£9.99	Villages of Kent (pb)	1-85937-294-5	£9.99
Norwich (pb)	1-85937-194-9	£8.99	Villages of Sussex (pb)	1-85937-295-3	£9.99
Nottingham (pb)	1-85937-324-0	£9.99	Warwickshire (pb)	1-85937-203-1	£9.99
Nottinghamshire (pb)	1-85937-187-6	£9.99	Welsh Castles (pb)	1-85937-322-4	£9.99
Oxford (pb)	1-85937-411-5	£9.99	West Midlands (pb)	1-85937-289-9	£9.99
Oxfordshire (pb)	1-85937-430-1	£9.99	West Sussex	1-85937-148-5	£14.99
Peak District (pb)	1-85937-280-5	£9.99	West Yorkshire (pb)	1-85937-201-5	£9.99
Penzance	1-85937-069-1	£12.99	Weymouth (pb)	1-85937-209-0	£9.99
Peterborough (pb)	1-85937-219-8	£9.99	Wiltshire (pb)	1-85937-277-5	£9.99
Piers	1-85937-237-6	£17.99	Wiltshire Churches (pb)	1-85937-171-x	£9.99
Plymouth	1-85937-119-1	£12.99	Wiltshire Living Memories	1-85937-245-7	£14.99
Poole & Sandbanks (pb)	1-85937-251-1	£9.99	Winchester (pb)	1-85937-428-x	£9.99
Preston (pb)	1-85937-212-0	£9.99	Windmills & Watermills	1-85937-242-2	£17.99
Reading (pb)	1-85937-238-4	£9.99	Worcester (pb)	1-85937-165-5	£9.99
Romford (pb)	1-85937-319-4	£9.99	Worcestershire	1-85937-152-3	£14.99
Salisbury (pb)	1-85937-239-2	£9.99	York (pb)	1-85937-199-x	£9.99
Scarborough (pb)	1-85937-379-8	£9.99	Yorkshire (pb)	1-85937-186-8	£9.99
St Albans (pb)	1-85937-341-0	£9.99	Yorkshire Living Memories	1-85937-166-3	£14.99

See Frith books on the internet www.francisfrith.co.uk

FRITH PRODUCTS & SERVICES

Francis Frith would doubtless be pleased to know that the pioneering publishing venture he started in 1860 still continues today. A hundred and forty years later, The Francis Frith Collection continues in the same innovative tradition and is now one of the foremost publishers of vintage photographs in the world. Some of the current activities include:

Interior Decoration

Today Frith's photographs can be seen framed and as giant wall murals in thousands of pubs, restaurants, hotels, banks, retail stores and other public buildings throughout the country. In every case they enhance the unique local atmosphere of the places they depict and provide reminders of gentler days in an increasingly busy and frenetic world.

Product Promotions

Frith products are used by many major companies to promote the sales of their own products or to reinforce their own history and heritage. Frith promotions have been used by Hovis bread, Courage beers, Scots Porage Oats, Colman's mustard, Cadbury's foods, Mellow Birds coffee, Dunhill pipe tobacco, Guinness, and Bulmer's Cider.

Genealogy and Family History

As the interest in family history and roots grows world-wide, more and more people are turning to Frith's photographs of Great Britain for images of the towns, villages and streets where their ancestors lived; and, of course, photographs of the churches and chapels where their ancestors were christened, married and buried are an essential part of every genealogy tree and family album.

Frith Products

All Frith photographs are available Framed or just as Mounted Prints and Posters (size 23 x 16 inches). These may be ordered from the address below. From time to time other products - Address Books, Calendars, Table Mats, etc - are available.

The Internet

Already twenty thousand Frith photographs can be viewed and purchased on the internet through the Frith websites and a myriad of partner sites.

For more detailed information on Frith companies and products, look at these sites:

www.francisfrith.co.uk
www.francisfrith.com
(for North American visitors)

See the complete list of Frith Books at:

www.francisfrith.co.uk

This web site is regularly updated with the latest list of publications from the Frith Book Company. If you wish to buy books relating to another part of the country that your local bookshop does not stock, you may purchase on-line.

For further information, trade, or author enquiries please contact us at the address below:
The Francis Frith Collection, Frith's Barn, Teffont, Salisbury, Wiltshire, England SP3 5QP.
Tel: +44 (0)1722 716 376 Fax: +44 (0)1722 716 881 Email: sales@francisfrith.co.uk

See Frith books on the internet www.francisfrith.co.uk

TO RECEIVE YOUR **FREE** MOUNTED PRINT

Mounted Print
Overall size 14 x 11 inches

Cut out this Voucher and return it with your remittance for £1.95 to cover postage and handling, to UK addresses. For overseas addresses please include £4.00 post and handling. Choose any photograph included in this book. Your SEPIA print will be A4 in size, and mounted in a cream mount with burgundy rule line, overall size 14 x 11 inches.

Order additional Mounted Prints at HALF PRICE (only £7.49 each*)

If there are further pictures you would like to order, possibly as gifts for friends and family, purchase them at half price (no additional postage and handling required).

Have your Mounted Prints framed*

For an additional £14.95 per print you can have your chosen Mounted Print framed in an elegant polished wood and gilt moulding, overall size 16 x 13 inches (no additional postage and handling required).

---

* IMPORTANT!
These special prices are only available if ordered using the original voucher on this page (no copies permitted) and at the same time as your free Mounted Print, for delivery to the same address

---

Frith Collectors' Guild

From time to time we publish a magazine of news and stories about Frith photographs and further special offers of Frith products. If you would like 12 months FREE membership, please return this form.

Send completed forms to:
The Francis Frith Collection, Frith's Barn, Teffont, Salisbury, Wiltshire SP3 5QP

Voucher for **FREE** and Reduced Price Frith Prints

Picture no.	Page number	Qty	Mounted @ £7.49	Framed + £14.95	Total Cost
		1	**Free of charge***	£	£
			£7.49	£	£
			£7.49	£	£
			£7.49	£	£
			£7.49	£	£
			£7.49	£	£

Please allow 28 days for delivery	*** Post & handling** **£1.95**
Book Title	**Total Order Cost** **£**

Please do not photocopy this voucher. Only the original is valid, so please cut it out and return it to us.

I enclose a cheque / postal order for £ . . . .
made payable to 'The Francis Frith Collection'
OR please debit my Mastercard / Visa / Switch / Amex card
(credit cards please on all overseas orders)

Number . . . .

Issue No(Switch only) . . . . .Valid from (Amex/Switch) . . . .

Expires . . . . Signature . . . .

Name Mr/Mrs/Ms . . . .

Address . . . .

. . . .

. . . . Postcode . . . .

Daytime Tel No . . . .   Valid to 31/12/02

The Francis Frith Collectors' Guild

Please enrol me as a member for 12 months free of charge.

Name Mr/Mrs/Ms . . . .

Address . . . .

. . . .

. . . .

. . . . Postcode . . . .

Would you like to find out more about Francis Frith?

We have recently recruited some entertaining speakers who are happy to visit local groups, clubs and societies to give an illustrated talk documenting Frith's travels and photographs. If you are a member of such a group and are interested in hosting a presentation, we would love to hear from you.

Our speakers bring with them a small selection of our local town and county books, together with sample prints. They are happy to take orders. A small proportion of the order value is donated to the group who have hosted the presentation. The talks are therefore an excellent way of fundraising for small groups and societies.

Can you help us with information about any of the Frith photographs in this book?

We are gradually compiling an historical record for each of the photographs in the Frith archive. It is always fascinating to find out the names of the people shown in the pictures, as well as insights into the shops, buildings and other features depicted.

If you recognize anyone in the photographs in this book, or if you have information not already included in the author's caption, do let us know. We would love to hear from you, and will try to publish it in future books or articles.

Our production team

Frith books are produced by a small dedicated team at offices in the converted Grade II listed 18th-century barn at Teffont near Salisbury, illustrated above. Most have worked with the Frith Collection for many years. All have in common one quality: they have a passion for the Frith Collection. The team is constantly expanding, but currently includes:

Jason Buck, John Buck, Douglas Burns, Heather Crisp, Isobel Hall, Rob Hames, Hazel Heaton, Peter Horne, James Kinnear, Tina Leary, Hannah Marsh, Eliza Sackett, Terence Sackett, Sandra Sanger, Shelley Tolcher, Susanna Walker, Clive Wathen and Jenny Wathen.